# This Journal Belongs To

_____

## Date

_____

# Crystals

## Journal

Crystals Journal

Hardback Edition

ISBN: 978-1-7343258-4-3

Published By:
Rebecca at the Well Foundation
https://www.RATW.org

Printed in the United States of America

# Moon Phases & Planetary Influences

# Moon Phases
## & Planetary Influences

# Moon Phases & Planetary Influences

# Moon Phases
# & Planetary Influences

# Moon Phases & Planetary Influences

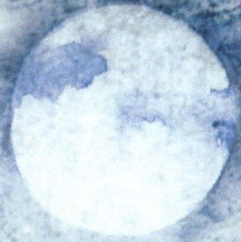

# Moon Phases & Planetary Influences

# Moon Phases & Planetary Influences

# Moon Phases & Planetary Influences

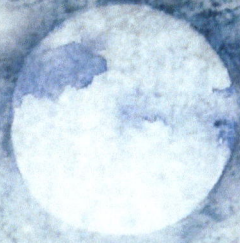

# Moon Phases & Planetary Influences

# Moon Phases & Planetary Influences

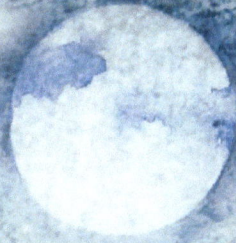

# Moon Phases
# & Planetary Influences

# Moon Phases & Planetary Influences

www.ingramcontent.com/pod-product-compliance
Lightning Source LLC
Chambersburg PA
CBHW040750150426
42813CB00060B/2896